Mrs Gillian M Peake
28 Damgate Lane

CW00543254

MY LIFE – MY PRAYER

The Autobiography of St Teresa of Avila for everyone

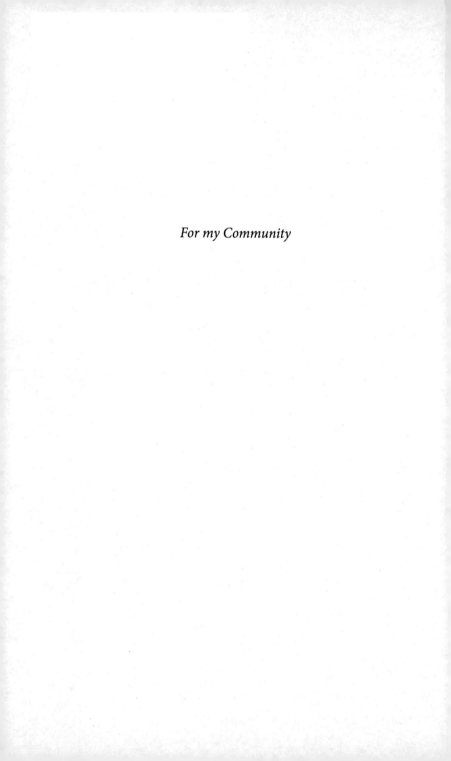

For my Community

MY LIFE – MY PRAYER

The Autobiography of St Teresa of Avila for everyone

Simplified and illustrated by
Elizabeth Ruth Obbard

New City

First published in 2017
in Great Britain by
New City

© 2017 Elizabeth Ruth Obbard

© Illustrated by Elizabeth Ruth Obbard

Graphic editor Sandy Bartus

British Cataloguing-in-Publication Data:
A catalogue record for this book is available from the
British Library

ISBN 978-1-905039-30-2

Typeset in Great Britain by
New City, London

Printed and bound by Books Factory

CONTENTS

INTRODUCTION

Who was Teresa of Avila? In 'The Book of her Life' she tries to give us an answer in her own words by recounting her early years and middle age, up to the time of the founding of the monastery of St Joseph. Teresa writes not just about her outward life but her interior journey, and those who helped her to grow in the love of God. It also records her experience of what held her back from making progress, and what drove her to reform the Carmelite Order to which she belonged and is in many ways its crowning glory.

Teresa is the kind of woman who would have made her mark on life no matter how she chose to live it. She was very much an individual – in Jungian terminology a self-actuated woman – well balanced, humorous, gifted with immense courage and foresight, no respecter of persons, mother and foundress not only of the Discalced Carmelite nuns but of the men's branch of the Order as well. Yet her early years gave little hint of what lay ahead – as writer, teacher, contemplative, one who was given wholly to God in her chosen vocation.

Teresa de Ahumada was born in 1515, the third child of her father's second marriage. It was a large family with two children from the first marriage and ten from the second. Her grandfather, Juan Sanchez, had been a forcibly converted Toledan Jew who had relapsed into the practice of his ancestral faith. For this he and his young sons had done public penance in Toledo Cathedral, paraded in the infamous 'sanbenitas' (yellow hooded penitential garments) for all to see. The youngest son was Alonso, Teresa's future father. This background was kept secret for a long time and only revealed by recent research into Teresa's lineage. It explains why she was so secretive about her heritage and why she was always ready to accept those of 'converso' blood into her monasteries. It also reminds us how careful she had to be with her writings; the Inquisition was not kind to those who were of 'tainted heritage'.

After the humiliation of Toledo, the Sanchez family moved to Avila and in due course Alonso married a pure blooded Castilian woman of 'old Christian' stock and adopted her name. He also managed to get a certificate attesting to his right to the title of 'hidalgo' or Spanish nobleman, an honour officially barred to those of mixed ancestry.

As a child Teresa was beautiful, vivacious, surrounded by adoring brothers; a typical child of a loving, wealthy and cultured home, assured of a brilliant marriage when she reached the required age.

Then Teresa's world was turned upside down. Her mother died giving birth to Teresa's only full sister, Juana, and the motherless girl found herself adrift. She was rising fourteen, and with her new found independence, she embarked on a mildly wild adolescence, at least as far as was compatible with the extreme vigilance Spaniards exercised over unmarried daughters, jealous at all costs to preserve the family honour. Teresa flirted with a cousin, enjoyed caring for her hands and hair, flaunted her rich clothes and jewels. Alonso turned a blind eye, for he idolised his favourite child. But at length, when her older half-sister Maria married, it was considered inappropriate for Teresa to remain alone at home, and she was sent to board with some Augustinian nuns who had a school attached to their convent. It was while there that Teresa considered the possibility of becoming a nun herself.

Teresa admits that she felt no attraction to marriage; she did not fancy being subject to anyone, or being kept confined and supervised in her husband's house as was common practice. She had seen her own mother fading away at thirty three, already old from ceaseless childbearing. Teresa wanted to avoid a similar fate, and yet she felt no attraction to the religious life either. In the end, after a spell of ill health and gentle persuasion from a pious uncle who pressed spiritual books on her, she decided she must force herself to enter a convent as there was no real alternative available.

Rather than join the nuns who had educated her, Teresa chose to apply to the Carmelite Convent of the Incarnation because, she admits disarmingly, she had a friend there and the life was not too strict. At twenty one, braving her father's disapproval, she and a brother crept out of the house early on All Souls Day; he to enter the Dominicans, she the Carmelites, where the community received her gladly. It was a large convent of about two hundred inhabitants, including not just nuns but friends and servants too. Many of the nuns came from the best Avilese families. Those with money were well provided for; those who were poor often went without the most basic necessities.

Faced with a 'fait accompli' Teresa's father accepted the inevitable. He settled a good dowry on his daughter, provided an annuity, and paid for a suite of rooms, including a private kitchen, oratory, parlour and guest room. If his favourite daughter was to be a nun, let her at least be so in keeping with her social status.

Teresa now embarked on a very ambivalent period of her life which was to last nearly twenty years. Yes, she had strong mindedly said that she wanted to be a nun and now she was one. She was a young woman of honour, but the standards of the convent were low and she was left without proper guidance or discipline.

Teresa wanted to pray, but other attractions were well nigh overwhelming. She was close to home and family for visits, extremely attractive, and much in demand in the parlour and at her friends' houses. Even her burgeoning spiritual gifts proved a trap in that they drew other people to her who admired her and wished to learn from her how to pray. They kept Teresa talking rather than recollected. Besides, her notoriously bad health (most likely psychosomatic in origin as she seemed to suffer from numerous unidentified illnesses) prevented her giving herself unreservedly to God – or so she persuaded herself. The convent of the Incarnation did not observe enclosure, there was no formal apostolate of education or nursing, and Teresa had nowhere constructive to use her energies. She was torn between observance of the Rule and pleasure. When at prayer, she watched the hourglass impatiently so that she could get back to the parlour. When in the parlour, she felt guilty about not praying enough. That did not prevent her from making great progress in prayer nevertheless. While ill she had read Francis de Osuna's 'Third Spiritual Alphabet' and set out on the path prescribed by the Franciscan author with good results, God aiding her with special graces despite her mediocrity in other areas.

At last, in her late thirties, this double mindedness came to an end as Teresa knelt before an image of the wounded Christ and begged for the grace to give herself completely to him. Her prayer was answered and a new era began for her. With the encouragement of a young cousin who asked her if she would provide a proper environment for those beginning a religious way of life, Teresa, rather reluctantly be it said, determined to found a convent of her own. There the Rule of Carmel would be kept strictly, in the manner of the first hermits who had settled on the holy mountain in the twelfth century, yet adapted to women of sixteenth century Spain.

It seemed a mad idea; yet Teresa found a firm supporter in Peter of Alcantara, a discalced Franciscan reformer, and a spiritual friend in St Clare of Assisi. It seems that her desire for a life of simplicity, poverty and prayer found an echo in the Franciscan ideal; yet when seeking the advice of learned men she turned to Dominicans and the newly founded Jesuits. Teresa was ready to accept help wherever she could find it.

Backed by a few friends and in great secrecy, Teresa prepared her first convent dedicated to St Joseph, who she chose as principal patron of this new venture. Her nuns would be 'hermits in community' in small, family style groups where strict enclosure ensured a desert atmosphere. There was to be no extensive property, a simple liturgy, and the sisters would work for a living. Neither was a family surname to be used which might highlight social class (or Judaic roots). All were to be equal.

Teresa began her first foundation at the age of forty seven, so she was designing a life based on her own mature reflection and personal experience. She was no young idealist but well into late middle age. From then on, and into old age, her life was spent travelling round and founding convents throughout Spain (although the book of her 'Life' ends with the founding of St Joseph's when her life's work was just beginning after many years of preparation). Young women flocked to her, since what she offered opened horizons for them that they would not otherwise experience – self-government, good human relationships in community, a measure of solitude, safety from outside interference, and intellectual input from learned churchmen. Some of Teresa's first prioresses were among the most gifted women of their generation. In forming her sisters Teresa was willing to be patient and loving, for she understood the gradual nature of the growth process. She knew human weakness from her own experience and the harm attendant on misguided forcefulness in spiritual direction.

For the next twenty years Teresa was to spend her life

making her ideals a reality. She was involved in business transactions, a huge apostolate of letter writing, and ceaseless negotiations. She had to face criticism and persecution from within and without the Order. She withstood it all in the certainty that she was doing God's work. She was, in fact, the first person to see prayer as an apostolate in itself, a gift for the whole Church, not just a way to personal sanctification.

Teresa wrote her books at the request of her sisters or her confessors, masterpieces of teaching on the interior life, full of acute psychological observations and humorous anecdotes. When she died as an old woman on the feast of St Francis 1482 she was sick, tired, yet still in good spirits as her life haemorrhaged away from cancer of the womb. 'Madre' inquired the provincial pompously, 'Where would you like to be buried?' 'Good gracious' she quipped, 'Can you not spare me here a little earth?' Then she turned, placed her head in the arms of her beloved infirmarian, Anne of St Bartholomew, and died.

The Book of her Life

Teresa's first book, that of her 'Life' was written at the request of her confessor and was meant to sing the mercies of the Lord towards her, she who had had to walk such a long and tortuous path to spiritual maturity. She also had to be clear about her orthodoxy, and her respect for the

Church and its teaching.

Teresa strives to be completely open about her many mistakes and sins along the way, and reveals a great openness about her experiences in prayer, for she realised that this way of 'living and acting in the truth' was her greatest safeguard. Also, as a woman, she was well aware that many men thought that, for women, prayer should be restricted to the saying of vocal prayers, anything more might lead the ignorant astray.

When Teresa began writing the book of her 'Life' she was fifty. She had not yet met John of the Cross (which she did two years later once her foundations began to multiply). The book weaves together teaching on prayer, personal experience of mystical graces, and factual events connected to her youth and early religious life.

The description of the 'Four Waters of Prayer' is her first attempt to systematise her understanding of how the life of prayer progresses. As such it does not reflect her most mature teaching found in the 'Interior Castle' or her practical advice for beginners as outlined in 'The Way of Perfection.' But the liveliness of the writing, and the disarming way Teresa charts the course of her spiritual development have a charm and directness that are hard to match. She also exhibits, in her description of the founding of St Joseph's, something of the qualities that would make her famous as a foundress: practical astuteness and a way of 'getting her way' despite obstacles.

Unfortunately the manuscript, or one of its copies, came to the attention of a benefactor, the Princess of Eboli, who insisted on reading it and then let it be circulated among her servants and acquaintances, who ridiculed Teresa on its account. When the princess, who insisted on trying her vocation in one of Teresa's monasteries after the death of her husband, made herself so obnoxious she had to be dismissed, she retaliated by denouncing the book to the Inquisition. Fortunately it fell into the hands of Fr Banes, one of Teresa's confessors who gave it his approval, but the work was withdrawn from circulation. This made Teresa turn her hand to more writing to make up for the loss. Inadvertently the Princess of Eboli did the world a favour!

Note

The 'Life' is a substantial manuscript, the original now in El Escorial (near Madrid) resting beside an original copy of St Augustine's 'Confessions', a book which influenced her in youth, and a volume of St John Chrysostom's – three Doctors of the Church together. How Teresa would have laughed at finding her book in such illustrious company!

I have tried to keep Teresa's conversational style in this simplified and edited edition, and have also cut out a number of experiences she described, keeping only what I consider the most significant. However, I think that the kernel of her work is here and in it you will meet this great woman who has influenced the Church ever since her death, and who lives in her daughters of Carmel even today.

ONE OF A BIG FAMILY

BEGINNINGS

Childhood and youth

I was the child of God-fearing and good parents. There were three sisters and nine brothers in all, from my father's two marriages. One brother was my favourite and we used to play at courting martyrdom or being hermits. With other girls I innocently pretended to be living in a monastery. I liked to pray too, especially the rosary, which my mother had taught me. She died when I was twelve years old, and I asked Mary to be a mother to me. Mine was a happy childhood, although I did not profit from it as much as I should have, as you will hear.

As I grew older I developed a taste for reading novels, a pastime I learned from my mother who read romantic stories to enable her to cope with her hard life of continual childbearing. Then I began to dress in fine clothes, wear jewellery, and take care of my hands and hair. After my mother's death I made friends with a cousin who encouraged me in frivolous pastimes, although I was wise enough not to compromise my honour. Parents, learn from my experience and watch over your children carefully – it is so easy to get diverted by bad companions as I was. And I was my father's favourite daughter too!

Anyway, when my older sister married and left home, my father felt I should be placed in a good school out of harm's way, and so I was sent to some Augustinian nuns as a boarder.

After the first eight days at school, during which I felt miserable, I started to like being there, and I became friendly with some of the nuns who were all very good. One nun was in charge of our dormitory and she told me about her own decision to be a nun, which came through reading the words

of the Gospel 'Many are called but few are chosen'. Gradually, under this sister's influence, I started to think about heaven and to wonder if, despite my repugnance for the religious life, I should become a nun myself. I have to say too that the vocation of marriage held no appeal for me either.

I didn't consider entering the Augustinian convent as it seemed to me that some of the penitential practises there were rather extreme. A friend of mine was a member of the Carmelite convent of the Incarnation, so if I were to become a nun I thought I would join that community.

Gradually I became interested in God; but at the end of my schooling I became so ill I was sent to live for a while with my married sister. She and her husband liked me very much and did all they could for me. Indeed, God let me be loved wherever I went – a gift that was undeserved yet has stood me in good stead in so many ways.

An uncle who was a widower then invited me to stay with him for a few days. He spent a lot of time in spiritual reading and prayer, but I have to say I wasn't particularly interested in reading the books he pressed on me. However, I gradually realised that the life of a nun would be to my advantage, for it seemed a way to avoid purgatory and get to heaven in the long run. My father wasn't at all pleased about this and refused his consent, so I persuaded a brother of mine to join a religious order too. We left home secretly very early one morning, and I felt the separation from my family so keenly I thought every bone in my body was being wrenched out of place.

LIFE IN THE CONVENT OF THE INCARNATION

Early adjustment and increasing ill health

In actual fact, once I was in the religious habit I discovered a great happiness welling up inside me. Everything in the convent delighted me, even sweeping the floor seemed far better than spending hours dressing up in the fine clothes I used to wear. Yes, my determination paid off, and I have discovered since then that just by making up one's mind and showing a determined determination to do something, one finds one is able to do far more than one at first realises, and even do it with a glad heart.

There was one nun who had a serious illness compounded by abdominal obstructions. Rather than being afraid of her I only desired to be as patient as she was. I saw that illness could be used by God for our good, and so I asked God to give it to me too if it would help me grow closer to him.

God heard my prayer, for the change in food and lifestyle affected my health and I did indeed become ill, remaining subject to fainting fits and weakness for the first year; and within two years I was so sick I needed to go away for treatment in the hope of a cure. I went to stay with my sister again, and also spent some time with the uncle I have already mentioned. He gave me a book called 'The Third Spiritual Alphabet'. I took this book as my guide and

began to practice recollection, to confess frequently, and to spend time in solitude. Yes, prayer began to be a delight to me, although I still had a long way to go.

My usual way of praying at this time was to look at Jesus as if present within me. I couldn't use my imagination or do much thinking, but I did find it helpful to have a book with me to help calm my mind. Prayer was dry, that is why reading was such a great help. In fact for eighteen years I never went to prayer without having a book to keep me focussed. Most beginners will need this kind of help so do not be discouraged.

As time went on no cure seemed to be taking place despite terrible purges and strong medicines. My constitution could not cope with the harsh treatment. I became unable to eat, all shrivelled up, with my nervous system giving me unbearable pain. My father brought me to other doctors, but eventually I felt I was close to death. So did those around me, for when I recovered consciousness I found wax on my eyes, such as they put on corpses. My grave had been dug in the Convent and the funeral rites had already been celebrated elsewhere by some friars.

I lived, but my tongue had been bitten to pieces, I could swallow nothing, and I remained paralysed and in severe pain. I asked to be brought back to the convent anyway, despite being so pitiably weak. The paralysis lasted over three years, only gradually getting better. When I could go about on my hands and knees rather than being carried in a sheet, I praised God! What is more, others were amazed at my patience and the way I was able to speak of God even in the midst of all this. I had attained the same patience as the nun I had admired before.

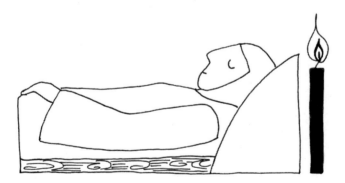

Growing attraction to prayer

This period of quiet gave me a longing to pray and spend time in solitude, and I enjoyed speaking about God if I could find someone of like mind. Yes, love grew in me even as my body knew pain and diminishment, although I would like to have been well in order to serve God better.

God granted me favours in prayer, so I began to understand what it meant to love him. One new virtue I acquired was that I never spoke ill of anyone, avoided all fault finding, and would not say anything about another that I would not want said about me. Gradually those who associated with me realised that when they were with me there would be no backbiting and gossip.

I still wanted solitude and liked to speak of God with others, even finding happiness in God-talk rather than the coarse speech of the worldly-wise. I read good books, confessed and communicated regularly, and tried to avoid sin, returning swiftly to repentance and God's grace whenever I failed. God was good to me although I did not serve him as well as I should.

At this time I took St Joseph to be my special friend and guide; I don't ever remember asking him for anything he did not obtain for me. After all, Jesus did what St Joseph asked him when he was on earth, so I trusted he would do the same in heaven. St Joseph is also a great teacher of prayer. Ask him to help you and you will discover this truth. No wonder that I resolved to celebrate his feast with special solemnity.

I TOOK ST JOSEPH AS MY SPECIAL FRIEND

I had asked for health, but when I had it I would have done better to remain sick as you shall hear.

Recovery and aftermath

Feeling better, I began to go from one pastime to another, so I soon lost my focus and quickly became bored with trying to pray and please God in all things. I was even tempted to stop praying and just say the prayers I was obliged to say vocally, while foregoing mental prayer altogether. Of course I kept up the appearance of a good religious and was never knowingly hypocritical, but that is no excuse.

That others did not see my faults was due to the fact that, even though I was young, people saw me withdrawing into solitude, wanting to be devout, loving sacred images, and never engaging in fault finding. Indeed, my superiors had such confidence in me they gave me more freedom than nuns much older than myself. My own monastery was a good one, but even so I had more freedom than was good for me. When I think how easy it is to follow the path of mediocrity in religious life I am not surprised that there is so much evil in the Church. God help us all!

I had many visitors, many friends, and liked to spend time with them. One person in particular was not good for me. Christ appeared to me one day when I was with this person and made me understand my blindness in the matter. I saw Christ with the eyes of my soul, not my body. Twenty six years have gone by and I still remember the impression left on me. A relative in the convent spoke to me about the danger I was in, but I did not believe her, and was annoyed at her impertinence in trying to correct me. I write this to warn others. Don't get entangled in useless and dangerous friendships. They are not good for anyone, however holy.

EARLY STEPS IN PRAYER

Temptations of beginners – Teresa speaks from experience

I had the greatest desire to help others improve – can you believe it! Beginners often have this fault although in this particular case it turned out well. I loved my father and wanted him also to gain the benefits of prayer, so I began to give him books for this purpose, and he made such progress in prayer and virtue that he became totally abandoned to God's will. He used to come and see me to talk about prayer and I felt too ashamed to tell him that I had abandoned the practice – I gave illness as my excuse and the duties of attending in Choir. However, there is no adequate excuse for giving up prayer, for it is an exercise of love, and love can be practised everywhere and by everyone. Solitude is not necessary.

Later I was with my father when he died. I took care of him during his last illness even though I was unwell myself at the time. He said that he suffered from great pain in his shoulder and I suggested that he remember our Lord carrying his cross, and this comforted him. My father was everything to me. In losing him I was totally bereft, but I hid my own grief so as to take care of him better while he still lived.

I helped other persons too, but deep down I knew I was living a double life, and this made me unhappy and uneasy. God was calling me on the one hand, and yet the world was also calling me and I felt totally torn. I went on like this for many years, a slave rather than the mistress of my own spirit. And yet the Lord hid my faults from others and let me be esteemed everywhere.

Let me give you some advice and suggest that if you want to pray you seek out good friends who will support and help you, and tell you the truth about yourself. I had many so-called 'friends' to walk with when I was going in the wrong direction, and none when I wanted to rise up again and take the right path. Find the kind of friends who will help you rise rather than fall, and you will grow strong.

The benefits of prayer

I sailed on this tempestuous sea of double-mindedness for twenty years, alternately falling and rising, I was neither happy with my worldly ways nor happy at my prayer. How I could have gone on like this even for a month, never mind all those years, I just don't know! But God mercifully allowed me never to forsake prayer completely, even though I needed a lot of courage to persevere as my soul was in perpetual conflict. I tell you all this so that you may praise God for his patience and his mercy to me. Yes, I tell you too, that persevering in prayer, even when your life isn't all that it should be, is worthwhile. God will eventually bring you safely to harbour as he brought me.

Never abandon prayer, I mean mental prayer. It is the remedy for all our ills. Always turn back to God no matter

MENTAL PRAYER · A LOVING CONVERSATION BETWEEN FRIENDS

what sins you commit, he is just waiting for your friendship to be reignited. I beg you, if you haven't begun to practice prayer, start now. Mental prayer is nothing else but a loving conversation between friends. So take time to be alone with God and benefit from his company.

ONLY 5 MORE MINUTES!

I just don't understand those who are afraid to practice prayer. The devil likes to make people afraid when there is nothing to be afraid of and everything to gain. Mental prayer means pondering on the Lord's life and all he has done for us, while reflecting on our own faults and how we might need to improve in the love and service of God. This was my own method of prayer at this time, even though I was often more distracted by thinking of how I wanted the assigned hour to be over, and listening for the clock to strike! It was such an effort to pray that it took courage to remain where I was. But sometimes, after making a great effort, I was rewarded with more quiet and delight than during the times when I had actually wanted to pray.

What are we afraid of? What are we waiting for? Prayer opens the door to God, even if our lives are not as good as they should be. And let prayer be coupled with reading, good friends and a delicate conscience. It is so easy to find people to encourage us to be careless and content with mediocrity.

I begged God to help me find true life. I wanted to live – but who would show me how?

The grace of conversion

Then it happened that one day I went into the oratory and saw there a statue that had been borrowed for the celebration of a special feast. It represented the wounded Christ, and I was so moved by it that my heart broke. I threw myself down before him in tears and begged him to strengthen me once and for all. From then on I believe I began to improve.

I was devoted to the glorious Magdalene and often thought about her conversion, especially at the time when I went to communion. I liked to ask this saint to pray for me and would place myself, like her, before the feet of Jesus, and weep tears of love and sorrow.

My method of prayer at this time was to try and picture Christ within me, especially in those Gospel scenes where he was most alone, like the garden of Gethsemane. I used to remain with him quietly as long as I could, despite distractions. Ever since I was a young nun I had begun to think of Jesus in the garden before going to sleep, and this practice remained with me over the years, as did making the sign of the cross before sleeping.

I did not find it easy to think about God, although some are adept at this. That is why I used a book to steady my thoughts. I also liked to look at nature – fields, water, flowers and so on. Nature reminded me of God the Creator's goodness and my own sins and ingratitude. I could not easily picture Christ although I was fond of images. If we love someone we like to see their picture often; and pictures of Christ can help recollection.

Reading is also a boon. At this time I read the Confessions of St Augustine and was profoundly moved by his story. Like me he had been a sinner, as had others, although they had only had to turn back to God once, while for me there was nothing but continual falling. However, I remembered

God's love for me, and so regained courage, and I trusted in his mercy no matter what transpired. I loved God but did not yet know how to respond to God's love in a practical way. Even so, I found myself turning away from things that might harm me, and growing in virtue.

We can help ourselves towards a tender love of God by recalling the passion of Jesus, his life and his sufferings. Stirring up love for love brings gladness of heart, even though we may shed some tears too. Praising God makes us aware of our sinfulness and nourishes the right sort of humility (more of that later). But we must be sure not to rely on our own strength and we must continue to serve God and grow in grace. We don't 'deserve' God's tender love. It is a free gift, so do not despise God's choice of you and the blessings that follow.

BEGINNING TO BE SERVANTS OF LOVE

THE FOUR WATERS OF PRAYER

Making a garden for God

I am now going to speak about those who are beginning to pray, I call them 'servants of love'. Just thinking about the dignity of this servitude delights me in a wonderful way. Loving God brings with it every blessing we could want, so why are we so dilatory in giving ourselves completely? Blessings so great are worth the effort involved. Goodness gracious! We want handfuls of God's love as well as lots of honour and praise for ourselves. No wonder our progress is often slow and laborious! So, be brave – little by little we can advance along the path trodden by Our Lord and come to union with him.

I will use the simile of making a garden for God. As beginners, God helps us clear the ground, pull up the weeds and plant some seeds that will make the garden beautiful and give joy to God the chief gardener. But without water a garden cannot flourish, and obtaining this water is the work of prayer as I shall describe. Water can be drawn from a well, which is hard work; or it can be obtained via an aquaduct or water wheel. Water may also come from a river or stream which irrigates the garden thoroughly; or it can come directly from heaven – straight from the hand of God, without any effort on our part.

The first water

Beginners in prayer are like those who draw water from a well. This involves a lot of work, and beginning to be a praying person demands a sustained effort. It means training ourselves to act in a recollected way, and being faithful to giving time to prayer no matter what we feel like. We have to grow in self-knowledge and that includes a knowledge of our sinfulness and weakness as well as our gifts.

With God's help we must do all we can to water the flowers (which are the virtues) in our garden, and cultivating

Prayer can be hard work

them takes time and effort. Our motive must be to please God and not ourselves, so we must keep trying to keep our thoughts on Christ and help him carry his cross. We are very much mistaken if we think prayer will be all sweetness and light. It takes courage to keep on keeping on... but be brave! The results are worth it in the long run. Don't compare yourself with others. God leads each according to the way he chooses and knows is best for the person concerned.

Temptations must be faced bravely. The devil likes to put people off praying, for he knows that they please God and save many others in the process. But be wise and gentle too. When necessary take a break: do some spiritual reading or work of charity. Go for a country walk, or talk to friends who are on the same path as you are. Do not be frightened by the cross, and remember that the Lord's yoke is sweet and his burden light. Do not try and force devotion or hanker after higher states of prayer. Wait on God's time, not your own. Walk with joy and freedom, not with a long face and a heavy heart.

A false humility may tempt us to give up and say we can't be like the great saints so what is the use of trying? True, we may not be able to do harsh penances and such like, but if we only go along at the pace of an ant, just doing a little and trying a little, we will get nowhere fast! Think of flying and realise that God wants us to fly high. We can all be saints – don't forget it! We should aim for the heights, desiring to be all we can be and giving God all we can give. That is the way to happiness. Stinginess and mediocrity drain our energy and make us miserable in the long run.

At prayer remain with Jesus in the Gospel stories and you will advance. Find what helps you most and seek advice from others who have followed this path, especially if they are learned and sensible. Another bit of advice: don't look at the faults of others but at their good qualities. It is easy for beginners to be judgemental and think they are advancing while others are going too slowly. Look to yourself and leave others alone. God is the judge, not you.

don't judge others

The second water

The second way to water the garden is by using a crank or water wheel. This means less work for the gardener, who is able to rest from time to time. This I take to refer to the prayer of quiet which I now want to discuss.

At this point we begin to be recollected. Grace is more evident in the way we live, and our will in prayer is 'held captive' by love. All this is something we cannot attain on our own, so we should accept God's gift of just being 'held' by him in loving attention without having to think all the time. We are like doves who may go looking for food, the food of thoughts and ideas, but find almost nothing, and so return to where they came from. In the same way we no longer go about searching for things to think about and pray about but can just rest quietly in God's presence.

In this state we are more open to just receiving the water God gives, and the flowers and plants in our garden begin to flourish. All we have to do is to say our 'Yes' to God's work in us. Deep down we experience a new happiness and delight which fills the void left by forsaking sin. However, in the spiritual life we are still beginners even if we feel interiorly peaceful and joyful, so do not trust in yourself – there is still a long way to go and God's grace is needed at every moment.

As this prayer of quiet is a gift, we cannot hold on to it by our own efforts, never mind 'straining at retaining' it ourselves, as if it were in our power to do so. However, we must realise the dignity of this state to which we have been

yes to GOD
in quiet trust

brought and not turn back to serious sin, as I did. Have a humble confidence in God, and if you fail do not abandon prayer in disgust but 'keep on keeping on' in order to win repentance and light. Then you can continue along the way with fortitude.

This prayer is a spark of true love enkindled by the Lord in our soul. And if we are faithful, this little spark will eventually turn into a great fire and profit many others in the process. What we must do during the prayer of quiet is to proceed gently, so that the little spark is not smothered by busy thinking. Leave thoughts alone. Stir up acts of love if need be, and remain humble. One act of humility is worth all the knowledge in the world, believe me! The soul does grow, but not like the body. A child automatically becomes an adult in due course, and the body then remains full grown and doesn't dwindle to smallness again. However, I have found that in prayer we may have to go back to basics, to 'smallness' when times are difficult. It helps to keep us humble and not trust in ourselves. Again, we should not have to go searching for ways to gain humility – incidents will arise naturally in the ordinary course of our life, and be more true than choosing 'humble' things that are artificial and out of character.

To sum up: the prayer of quiet is the beginning of all blessings. The flowers in our garden are starting to bud, and we know in our hearts that God is with us. But we must not trust in ourselves. Fear God in peacefulness and humility, accepting the pain that comes with deepening self-knowledge, which will be painful because based on truth.

* Praise * freedom *
* fruitfulness * love *

The third water

In the third water the garden is irrigated by means of a river or spring, so there is much less labour involved. In fact, the Lord himself becomes the principal gardener.

When at prayer the faculties 'go to sleep' and the waters of grace rise up so high that we are immobilised. We are like a dying person holding a candle with only a little time left before a longed-for death overtakes us, and the candle is snuffed out. This death I see as being a complete death to earthly things and an enjoyment of God even here on earth.

Five or six years ago the Lord gave me this kind of prayer, but then I did not know how to speak about it. All I knew was that it was not yet complete union, but certainly more than the prayer of quiet of the second water. In this third water the faculties are completely occupied with God. Praise just seems to burst from the heart, and one wants to share this joy with others. We are like the woman in the gospels who called in her neighbours to celebrate when she had found the lost coin, or like King David when he played the harp and sang the praises of God. I just love King David. I am devoted to him and want to see us all devoted to him too – especially those of us who are sinners.

Nothing can be compared to the delights the Lord wants our souls to enjoy in their exile. It is as if we were bearing a delicately wrought and extremely heavy cross: 'delicate' because it is pleasing, 'heavy' because it can seem we have no capacity to bear it, yet would not want to be without it, for basically we want nothing but the Lord. O dear! There are too may cautious preachers around who do not challenge their hearers to reach the heights; they are too afraid they might give offence by speaking out. Being themselves without the flame of love that galvanised the apostles onwards they do not enkindle love in their hearers, only complacency. We must be ready to lose and gain all for Christ. That is the way to freedom, the rest is mere slavery!

In this third water the flowers of the garden are really beginning to give out their fragrance, the water being given without measure. The fruits of the garden too grow and ripen in such a way that we can be sustained by them, and eventually, when we have grown strong, offer them to others.

The results of this third water are beyond anything we could achieve by our own efforts. We realise that we have changed, and are not only wrapt in prayer during prayer time, but able to study and serve as well, uniting the active with the contemplative life. Even in activity we are conscious of being with God in our deepest depths.

The fourth water

In the fourth water all the senses are occupied in a prayer that is accompanied by much glory and consolation, and it gives us a joy so deep that it cannot be communicated. I don't quite know how to explain all this since two separate beings, God and ourselves, become one. There is a union of love beyond words or concepts.

This heavenly water saturates and soaks the entire garden, but alas, seasons change and we cannot have permanent ease. If one kind of water is lacking we must take care

humility
gratitude
great desires

to obtain another. Water can come from heaven when the gardener is least expecting it, but at first it tends to come after an extended period of mental prayer. It is as if the Lord takes a tiny bird from one small move to another, until he places it in the nest where it can find repose. This is when God has seen the little bird flying around for a long time, striving to use all its faculties of thinking and loving, and making every effort to please God. The reward is certainly worth every trial.

Seeking God in earnest engenders a marvellous and gentle delight, very fleeting at first. Memory and imagination may cause inner disturbance but the will holds firm and focussed.

Thinking about this after communion and wanting to write about what the soul does during this prayer the Lord spoke these words to me: 'It detaches itself from everything, my daughter, so as to abide more in me. It is no longer the soul that lives but I. Since it cannot comprehend what it understands, there is an understanding in not understanding.' Whoever has experienced this prayer will know what I am saying, for the soul becomes truly united to God in a marvellous and mysterious way.

Of course such graces leave definite signs, such as the gift of tears, the waters of which just set the fire of love blazing ever more brightly. Also courage increases and humility becomes deeper. For just as the sun shows up cobwebs, so we can see more clearly how we sin and how God gives generously without our having deserved it. Vainglory flies out of the window. It is impossible to delight in self when we can see only God's glory and goodness permeating our littleness and meanness.

Now the fragrance of the flowers and the ripeness of the fruit in our garden attract others. Our soil is by now well cultivated by trial, persecution, criticisms, illnesses (few reach this stage without them) and is softened by our living in great detachment from self-interest. The water soaks in so that the ground is hardly ever dry. But should we become careless gardeners and forget gratitude to God for his gifts we may find ourselves with very hard and barren earth once more. So be careful! Fortunately we can always repent, for tears attract the water back again. So never be discouraged. Look at me and take my advice: when I abandoned prayer I was lost. Yet the Lord had mercy on me and raised me up again. By the power of the sacraments I was restored and healed.

When the soul has reached the higher stages of prayer, God gives the strength to put great desires into action, and it becomes clear that anything that is not pleasing to God is nothing and worth less than nothing – indeed completely useless.

And so my prayer has become like this:

> *Do you strengthen and prepare my soul first of all,*
> *good of all good my Jesus,*
> *and then ordain means whereby I may do something for*
> *you.*
> *For no one could bear to receive as much as I have done*
> *and pay nothing in return.*

Here is my life, my honour, my will, I am yours.
Dispose of me according to your desire.
I see clearly how little I am capable of by myself,
but I shall be able to do all things
provided that you withdraw not yourself from me.

SOME PRACTICAL ADVICE TO THOSE WHO ARE GROWING IN PRAYER

Never abandon the humanity of Christ

When people are advancing in prayer they are often told to rid themselves of all bodily images and just contemplate the Divinity. They even see the humanity of Christ as an obstacle to this contemplation. In support of this theory they quote the words of Jesus that the Holy Spirit will be with them to teach them everything. In their eyes the work of contemplation is entirely spiritual, and is about being immersed in the God who is everywhere.

But to withdraw one's thoughts completely from the person of Jesus in bodily form is something I cannot endure. At first I thought that the prayer of quiet involved turning aside from all images. What an ignoramus I was! Fortunately I always returned to the Lord, especially when receiving communion, and I desired to see a picture or image of him wherever I turned my eyes.

We need the companionship of Christ along our way, and so we must never try to get rid of him and enter some nebulous spiritual state. If we cannot always be thinking about the passion, then look at Jesus in his risen life, or as he was with the apostles. He never leaves us for a moment, so why should we leave him? Whoever lives in the presence of such a good friend and leader can endure all things. The Lord helps and strengthens us and never fails.

He is a true friend. I see clearly that if we want to please God and receive his favours they must come to us through the sacred humanity of Christ. Many, many times I have perceived this truth through experience. The Lord has told it to me. I have definitely seen that we must enter by this gate and no other.

NEVER ABANDON THE HUMANITY OF CHRIST

When I considered the saints like St Paul, St Anthony of Padua, St Francis, St Bernard, St Catherine of Siena and others, I saw that they too had always reverenced and loved Christ in his humanity. All blessings come through him. This is the way to go.

Christ is a good friend too in times of dryness, for we cannot get rid of our bodies and pretend to be angels. Wherever we are, and however we are feeling, seek the company of Christ and we cannot go wrong. Be simple and humble. Walk with Jesus and all will turn out well.

As often as we think of Christ we should recall the love he has for us, the gifts he has given us, and the pledges of his love, for love draws forth love in return. Wherever we are on the spiritual path let us try to awaken ourselves to love. For once the Lord has impressed this love upon our hearts all will become easy, and we shall carry out our tasks quickly and without much effort. May His Majesty give us love, demonstrated by the love borne us by the Son at such cost.

TERESA CONTINUES HER LIFE STORY

Personal favours granted by God

Returning to my life story is really about the new life that God granted me through following the path of prayer. It was a whole new life, a blessed life, a life quite different from my previous existence.

Once I started to pray, the Lord frequently gave me the prayer of quiet, but as I was so imperfect I began to consult learned people about my experiences; I was afraid that the devil might have a hand in what was going on. I was also aware that I had a number of attachments that might be wrong, so I resolved to strive after a very pure conscience.

I was put in touch with a holy priest, Gaspar Daza. He is well known as a spiritual director: mild, charming, and fostering all that is good. The man who recommended him to me was a married man of great perfection who had practised prayer for nearly forty years. His family and mine are connected through marriage.

Well, Gaspar Daza began to guide me as if I were already a strong woman, much stronger that I actually was, and so I took fright. I was ready to give up before I had hardly begun! Fortunately my married friend was wiser and humbler. He shared with me that he himself had had to go slowly at first, and that little by little God would accomplish his work in me too. However, my worst problem was that he thought I could not be favoured by God when my progress in virtue was so slow – he said the devil must have a hand in it. Also there was gossip about me and the favours I was receiving. I felt ashamed and afraid.

I was advised to speak to the Jesuits, and Father Diego de Cetina assured me that all was well. He was a very learned man and heard my general confession. He understood me and guided me well, making me devoted to the passion of Christ and his humanity. So I began to love the sacred humanity and to build my prayer on firm foundations. My conscience became more delicate and I found that if I was holding on to some bad habit I could not pray. I met Fr Francis Borgia, the former Duke of Gandia who had given up everything for God and entered the Society of Jesus. He listened to all I had to say and reassured me that I was led by the Spirit, and should not resist if I felt 'carried away' in prayer.

As my confessor was moved elsewhere I found another Jesuit who led me to greater perfection. He was also confessor to my friend Dona Guiomar de Ulloa. He advised me to recite the hymn 'Veni Creator' so that God would give me light about some attachments that I was finding hard to give up. Suddenly, while I was saying this prayer one day a rapture came upon me so suddenly that it carried me out of myself. It was the first time our Lord granted me the favour of rapture, and I heard these words: 'No longer do I want you to talk with people but with angels.' Yes, these words have since been fulfilled in that I can no longer bear a special love for anyone except those who love and serve God.

From that day on I was very courageous in abandoning all for God. My confessor had wisely waited until the right moment for the Lord to do this work in me. God himself gave me the freedom I had tried vainly to achieve by my own efforts for many years.

Free at last!

An exclamation of love

O wonderful kindness of God!
You, Lord, allow me to gaze on you
with eyes that have gazed on sinful things.
O all you who have begun to practice prayer
and have true faith,
what good things can you seek in this life
– leaving aside what is gained for eternity
– that could compare with the least of these favours!
Reflect, for it is true, that God gives himself to those who
give up everything for him.
God has no favourites. God loves everyone.
There is no excuse for anyone when God has been so
good to me.
The love and knowledge of God surpass anything we
could desire on earth, so let us help Jesus carry the cross.
If we want only glory and worldly honour we are on the
wrong path and shall never arrive at our goal.
What a joy for those who reach heaven knowing that,
even if they began late, they have refused God nothing.
How rich we will be to have left all riches for Christ.
How honoured we will be if we have not sought honour
in this world.
How wise we will be because we were not afraid to be
considered mad.
Yes, true wisdom lies in being a heroic lover of Christ!
Yet look at the reality we see around us.
We want to proceed only with great caution.

We are so careful to avoid giving scandal that we go slowly – even religious and priests proceed at this reluctant pace.

Yet we should be showing the zeal of the apostles, being on fire with love and courage, accomplishing great things for God!

Vision of a Seraph

Once when in an ecstasy I saw the following vision. Close to my left side there was an angel in bodily form. I don't usually see angels like this, rather they appear in intellectual visions without any 'seeing' with my eyes. However, this time the Lord wanted me to see the vision as I shall describe.

The angel was small, very beautiful, with a face aflame, seeming to be all on fire like the cherubim. In his hands was a large golden dart, and at the iron tip there seemed to be a little fire. The angel plunged this dart several times into my heart, reaching deep within me. When he drew it out I thought he was carrying off the deepest part of me, and he left me blazing with a great love of God. I was in such a mixture of spiritual pain and sweetness that even my body was affected.

May God be blessed forever for granting so many favours to one who responds so poorly to such great gifts as these.

St Peter of Alcantara

The great penitent and Franciscan friar, Peter of Alcantara, was someone sent to me by God through the goodness of the widow I have already mentioned, Dona Guiomar de Ulloa. She was one person who believed in me, and that what I was experiencing came from God.

Without telling me, she obtained permission for me to stay with her in her home for eight days so that I could talk with Friar Peter more easily. I opened my soul to him and we discussed many things together. Almost straight away I saw that he understood me for he had had similar experiences, and he reassured me that what was happening was the work of the Spirit. He also reassured my friends who had doubted the reality of what I had undergone in prayer.

We agreed to pray for each other and I undertook to write to him about my experiences as well as to continue confiding in my confessor. It seemed as if Friar Peter was a gift to me from St Joseph, and although I could not trust his words completely I was left very consoled.

The gift of living water

My troubles were not over but they were ameliorated. The devil likes us to live with disquiet and darkness. I had a false humility which tended to see the worst in myself, attributing blame where there was none. The devil represents justice, harshness, dryness, while God always wants us to trust in his mercy and never despair. True, I see myself as full of imperfections, but it seems to me that I really do love God, and I try to feed the fire of love continually, even pieces of straw help. Love is always stirring and thinking of what it can do to praise God and enable others to praise him, like water continually overflowing its banks.

Oh, how often do I recall the living water that the Lord told the Samaritan woman about. I am very fond of this Gospel passage and have been since my childhood, although I did not understand it then as I do now. I often begged our Lord to give me some of this water. I had a picture of the episode of the Lord at the well that hung where I could always see it, and which bore the inscription: 'Lord, give me some of this water.'

The problem of human respect

Being concerned about our good name, bothering about what others think of us, is a sure sign that we are far from perfect.

Sometimes I see people who do wonderful things for God. My word, why are they not already canonised saints! Ah, it is that fatal weakness – concern about our so-called 'honour'. We even think we are obliged to cultivate the good opinion of others as if that were part of serving God.

Well, believe me, I who am nothing but a little ant, if we do not remove this caterpillar of human respect, the tree may not be damaged completely but all the virtues will be worm eaten. The tree is not beautiful. It does not flourish or allow others to flourish in its vicinity, and the fruit of good example it bears is not healthy, nor is it long lasting. Even if we are only concerned about some small point of honour it is as if a note on the organ were out of tune – all the music becomes dissonant. What damage this does to the soul, and in the path of prayer it is pestilential!

Think of how Christ bore injuries and slander – and here we are wanting everyone to think well of us. Who do we think we are? If we want all our 'rights' and everyone's good opinion we are on the wrong road; it certainly isn't the road Christ took!

In my own life I discovered that being humble and admitting faults and difficulties was the first step to overcoming them, and it led me to interior freedom because I was living in the truth.

Teresa sees her place in hell

While I was in prayer one day I understood that our Lord wanted me to see the place that had been reserved for me in hell because of my sins. It was as if I were in a very long, narrow alleyway, like an oven. It was low and dark, foul smelling and swarming with horrible creatures. At the end of the alleyway was a hole like a small cupboard hollowed

out in the wall. I cannot even begin to describe what I felt like and the pains I endured.

This made me realise how important it is to pray and sacrifice for others, so that no one comes to this terrible place. It also convinced me of the preciousness of life and how we should do all we can while we live to give glory to God in everything.

The first thing I resolved was to live the life I had professed as a nun as perfectly as possible. I also realised that the convent I lived in was not all that conducive to prayer because the nuns went out and about so much, and the Rule was kept in a rather lax manner, even though there were many good sisters who lived there. And so my life began to take a new direction.

WHY NOT BECOME REFORMED NUNS?

A VOCATION AS FOUNDRESS EMERGES

The seed of an idea is sown

I was with friends one day in my room and it happened that while we were talking one of them said it would be good to become reformed nuns ('discalced' – where sandals or bare feet replaced the wearing of shoes as a sign of a stricter way of life). I had been having desires like this for some time, so I began to discuss it with that widow friend of mine, Dona Guiomar de Ulloa, who thought as I did on many things. And so plans got underway for a reformed house where the Rule would be strictly observed. On the other hand, I really liked the convent I was in; my rooms were as I wanted them and I enjoyed my life there, so I dragged my feet somewhat in getting things started. I just said I would pray about the matter meanwhile.

One day after communion the Lord earnestly asked me to put the plan into practice. He said he would be well served in the new house, and that it should be dedicated to St Joseph who would keep watch over one door while Our Lady kept watch over the other. I could not doubt that the Lord had spoken and so I felt compelled to go ahead even though I knew it would disturb my hard won peace. Dona Guiomar spoke with my provincial superior, Fr Angel Salazar, and this man gave me the necessary permission to proceed with my plans. I thought a small community of thirteen would be best, as then the sisters would really get to know one another and be friends. I also wanted an income to be provided so they would not be in want of anything. I wrote to Friar Peter of Alcantara telling him of my project, and he was enthusiastic about it.

Well! Hardly had the news of the proposed foundation got out than there was an uproar in the town! Who did I think I was? There was no need for another monastery when where I was was good enough for anyone! In the end the provincial was swayed by all this and wavered somewhat, but Dona Guiomar stood firm. Finally I felt sure I should go ahead anyway since the project was from God. A Dominican father who was consulted prayed about the matter and told me to just trust in God and act. Gradually others helped too.

Overcoming obstacles

All the plans were proceeding apace when the Provincial changed his mind. Looking back this was a stroke of Providence. People thought I was just a foolish woman with ideas above my station, but God was going to bring the work to completion in another and better way, as it eventually turned out.

As you can imagine the nuns in my own monastery thought I was insulting them and their way of life by wanting something more. Some even thought I should be put in the convent prison, but I remained silent about everything.

I knew I had done all that I could, and I never ceased believing that the foundation would come about in God's good time. So it was a shock when even my Jesuit confessor, Baltazar Alvarez, said it had all been a dream and I should obviously forget the whole thing. Had even my prayer been an illusion then? But the Lord in his own way consoled me and strengthened me, so I took no notice of the persecution and just bided my time.

In this way I realised how God strengthens and blesses those who suffer persecution for his sake. Some even warned me that I might be reported to the Inquisition, but I only laughed. I knew I had nothing to fear as I was so careful about everything to do with the Church and her ceremonies.

When a new rector came to the Jesuit house where my confessor lived, he came to see me. Suddenly I knew that this man understood me at a deep level and my soul opened out as I spoke. He was a man who knew how to encourage others and make them run rather than walk with measured step. After a lot of thought this man and my confessor realised that they should not put any obstacles in the way of the proposed foundation.

Now I knew I must proceed, but I had little money, few friends, and an unsympathetic Carmelite superior (so I left him in the dark about my plans). One house I looked at seemed too small for a monastery, yet at the Lord's bidding I looked at it more closely and, though small, saw it would be perfect for what I had in mind. Another time when I had no money to pay workmen St Joseph revealed that I would lack nothing essential so should hire them anyway.

One day after communion St Clare appeared to me and told me that she would help me continue the work I had begun. This is a saint I have grown to love, and her nuns have helped me in other ways too. Gradually the poverty St Clare espoused began to be mine too, and I found that if I trusted God I would be provided for.

The blessing of Our Lady

Some time later, on the feast of the Assumption, I saw Our Lady at my right side and St Joseph at my left clothing me in a beautiful white robe, by which I understood that I was

now cleansed of my sins. It seemed to me too that Our Lady took me by the hand and told me that I was making her very happy by serving St Joseph and that, together with Our Lord, they would watch over us. As a sign she placed a most beautiful jewelled cross around my neck, more beautiful than anything one could imagine or see on earth.

I cannot describe Our Lady except to say she was clad in a brilliant, yet soft, white robe, and was like a young girl. I did not see St Joseph clearly although I knew he was there.

Our Lady reassured me about my obedience not being given to the superior of the Order. That fact had distressed me to be sure, but Our Lord told me we should petition Rome in a certain way and this would get our request answered. And so it came about that my petition was granted. Later I was to see that it was indeed for the best that we gave our obedience to the bishop rather than the Order, but as yet I was still to meet the said prelate who would be strongly in favour of this foundation.

The Lord provides

Well, no matter how you try to keep things secret people hear about them. I was afraid someone would tell the Carmelite provincial and he would order me to desist. Fortunately the Lord saw to it that I had to leave Avila, and so was above suspicion as things went ahead in my absence.

It happened that a wealthy woman, Dona Luisa de la Cerda, who lived about twenty miles away in Medina, was grieving so much at the death of her husband that people feared for her health. She had heard about me and asked the provincial to let me stay with her and console her, and he ordered me to go. I arrived at her house on Christmas Eve.

True enough, this lady began to get better when I was with her, and she conceived a great liking for me. I also

realised from my experience with her that being rich and noble does not exempt anyone from trials and difficulties. In fact, people like her are often constrained by so much protocol in eating, drinking, what one wears, how one is addressed and so forth that life can be a real trial. There is nothing to envy at all, even though from the outside such a life may seem very easy and sweet, cushioned by plenty of money.

I did speak about the proposed foundation with a Dominican father and a few others under the seal of confession, and of how I wanted those I knew and loved to grow in perfection and God's service. Real experience of

God makes all the difference in discerning the right way to walk. Let those who think they are wise listen to this little old woman and be humble. The Dominican father I have mentioned learned many things from me that he had only known before through reading and study rather than by experience. Yes, the Lord has revealed to me things about several Jesuit and Dominican fathers and the progress they have made, and needed to make, before becoming great servants of God. And as I have grown from weakness to maturity so I have been able to help others. Suffering is a great teacher.

The observance of Holy Poverty decided upon

While I was with Dona Luisa (I stayed with her for a year and a half) Maria de Jesus, a 'beata' (a dedicated woman who wore a religious habit but without formal vows) came to see me. She too planned to found a reformed monastery of our Order at Alcala and she wanted to speak to me about it.

Maria was a woman of great penitence and prayer, and she already had letters from Rome giving her permission to carry out her plans. One of the things this woman pointed out to me was that our primitive Rule forbade ownership of anything. I had overlooked this point, and was intending that the nuns should have an income so as not to have any worries about their support. I had noticed that monasteries that were very poor and had to beg were often distracted by neediness; but on further reflection I realised that they were poor because they were distracted and not fervent religious. So I determined to rely on God and embrace a life of poverty, trusting the Lord would provide.

As expected there were lots of objections put forward, backed up of course by learned men with heads full of theology. I just said that I wasn't interested in all their theology, I just wanted to follow my vocation perfectly. Others were in favour of the proposal and then changed their minds. To them I said that I would stick with their first opinion thank you very much, and that was that! My friend invited that holy Franciscan Peter of Alcantara to the house and he supported me to the hilt. He knew from experience the blessings of a life of poverty. So I stopped looking for other opinions and went with his. In prayer Our Lord told me to go ahead: he willed the foundation and willed it in poverty.

The foundation becomes a reality

My monastery of the Incarnation was about to elect a superior and there were rumours that they might elect me. The provincial said I could choose whether or not to return to Avila, while the Lord told me to go anyway and accept the cross waiting for me. I thought the cross would be my election, which I certainly didn't want. In my inner turmoil prayer became very difficult, and I asked Dona Luisa to let me go. I had been promised a cross, but had no idea it would be as heavy as that which came my way, as you will hear. On the other hand I wanted to please and serve God, and if I could do this better, then suffering had to be accepted and even welcomed. Making God happy is ultimately the way to happiness for ourselves.

Once I left Medina I journeyed contentedly, with a firm resolve to do whatever God wanted. And lo and behold – the very night I reached Avila permission from Rome arrived for me to make my foundation. As the provincial was still in the dark about it all (and not approving), the bishop accepted to take us under his wing. He was a man who, despite his objection to my plans for a poor house, was fond of people who he saw were determined to serve the Lord. Friar Peter of Alcantara was also there and got others onto our side. It seems that God kept this dear man alive so that he could speak up for us, since a few days later he died.

Everything had to be completed in secret, otherwise nothing could have been accomplished. Fortunately at this point my brother in law became ill, and as his wife was

THE FIRST FOUR

away my superiors gave permission for me to go to him. Since he had bought the house for us and was living in it I was able to stay and supervise the repairs, renovations and adaptations that the workmen had to do. Then when everything was finished my brother in law got well again. How the ways of God leave me to marvel!

What with one thing and another I had to arrange everything in a hurry, and it was stressful enough for anyone to cope with. I thought this must be the cross I was expecting, but no, something far worse was in store. More of that later.

On St Bartholomew's Day, August 24th, everything was ready. The Blessed Sacrament was reserved, the bell rung, and four young women received the habit. This is a day to remember – the founding of the monastery of our most glorious father St Joseph on St Bartholomew's Day, 1562. I was in the outside chapel to see the ceremony, together with two of our nuns from the Incarnation. Everything had been done with due permission and advice from learned men. I felt happy and relieved that all was well, and that God's work had been accomplished despite my many imperfections.

Doubts and difficulties

About three or four hours after this happy occasion the devil put all sorts of doubts into my mind. Had I done the right thing? Had I been disobedient? I suspected, and rightly, that the provincial would be displeased with me. What if my sisters lacked food or other necessaries? I forgot all the good things that had happened, the prayers I had said, Our Lord's assurances, and became totally depressed. And what about myself? Did I really want to shut myself up in a small house like this when I had so many friends and plenty of space where I was? Dear God, how fickle our feelings are! One moment all happiness and the next all darkness! After some prayer before the Sacrament I resolved that I would, in due course, come and live at St Joseph's, no matter its drawbacks as I saw them. And with this strong resolve the

I HAD TO EXPLAIN MYSELF

devil fled, leaving me with a calm and peace that have since never deserted me.

The prioress of my monastery sent word that I was to return there at once. I knew I would be going through a hard time, but now the new house was established I didn't worry. I thought that if I was to be put in the prison I would at least get a good rest!

Fortunately after speaking with the prioress and the provincial with all due humility I was able to explain myself to their satisfaction. After all, I was working for the good of the whole Order, not personal profit.

Within a few days the whole city was in uproar about the new community, condemning me and complaining that the inhabitants of Avila could not support another religious house, there were too many already. A long lawsuit was begun to get the house to close; then they said that if I would accept an income they would tolerate it. However, I would not give way on this point. Then the holy Peter of Alcantara appeared to me in a dream and assured me that the Lord would be well served in this new monastery – I should hold out and trust God.

Ultimately all was settled and the house was allowed to continue. Meanwhile I was permitted to go there to teach the sisters the Divine Office and other ceremonies.

Teresa enters her new home and begins her new life

Before entering the new monastery, while in prayer outside the church, being almost in rapture, it seemed as if I saw Christ receiving me with great love, placing a crown on my head, and thanking me for all I had done for his mother. Later I saw the Mother of God in glory sheltering us all under her white mantle.

As soon as the liturgical offices were being celebrated people began to come to St Joseph's. More nuns were accepted (though I kept the initial number to thirteen) and those persons who had been most opposed began to provide us with all that we needed. Yes, we became a very happy little group, fervent in God's service, rejoicing in 'being

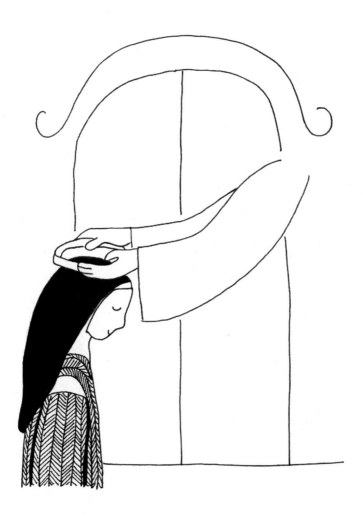

alone with Him alone,' which is the recipe for happiness and fervour.

A much greater love for and confidence in Our Lord began to grow in me when I saw Jesus as one with whom I could converse continually. I saw that he was truly human as well as being divine, and so I could speak to him as to a friend. On earth lords are difficult to approach and need all kinds of buttering up and careful treatment if we are to get what we want from them. But this Lord is someone we can come to with confidence at any time, and speak with in any way we like without standing on ceremony.

Sometimes the Lord will lead me into a rapture and I will 'see' a dove or the Virgin or something to do with the lives of others. I am also made aware of my weakness and sinfulness. Yes, you Lord sustain us little by little with your blessings, and you have even shown me people I know who have died and are now in the glory of heaven.

Once Christ appeared to me and began to show me the wound in his left hand, and with the other hand drew out a large nail that had been embedded in the flesh and which tore as he pulled it out. I felt much pity for the sharp pain. Meanwhile he told me that someone who had suffered such pain for me should not be doubted, and his love would grant all that I asked for. At other times Christ has spoken to me from the same picture of him at the pillar that we have in one of our hermitages where I have gone to pray. I have discovered that the Lord leads persons to prayer and the avoidance of sin simply because I have prayed for them. It is amazing! But in the end what matters are not visions but the effects seen in a life of loving self-giving, and that can take place when there are no special feelings at all. God gives grace as God wills and not as we think he should. I list some of God's favours but I cannot list them all – and all given freely and undeservedly to a sinner.

Now that I live in this house of St Joseph the Lord has been pleased to give me interior peace and I am not at all bothered by what people say or what may happen to me from now on.

FINAL RECOMMENDATION

To the revered Father Garcia de Toledo O.P. I give this manuscript. I have had little time to write all this but hope it will prove to be of benefit to someone, bringing others to praise the Lord, even if that were only one person, and even if afterwards the manuscript was burned. Please also show this to the three persons who have been my confessors.

May the Lord keep you in his hands and make you a great saint. My intentions in writing have been sincere and I have wanted to sing the Lord's mercies to me, sinner that I am.

May it please the Lord that my soul may not be lost which, with so many sacrifices, in so many ways, and so often, he has rescued from hell and brought to himself. Amen.

FOR FURTHER READING

TEXTS

Teresa of Avila, The Book of her Life; Volume 1 in Collected Works, Trans. K. Kavanagh & 0. Rodriguez, ICS Publications, 1976

Teresa of Avila, The Life of Holy Mother Teresa of Jesus; Volume I in Complete Works of St Teresa, Trans E. Allison Peers, Sheed & Ward, 1946

RELATED WORKS

Carrera, E.: *Teresa of Avila's Autobiography – Authority, Power and the Self in Mid-Sixteenth-Century Spain,* Legenda, 2005

Clissold, S.: *St Teresa of Avila,* Sheldon Press, 1979

Du Boulay, S.: *St Teresa of Avila,* Hodder and Stoughton, 1991

Luti, J.M.: *Teresa of Avila's Way,* Liturgical Press, 1991

Obbard, E.: *La Madre, The Life and Spirituality of St Teresa of Avila,* St Paul's, 1996

Slade, C.: *St Teresa of Avila, Author of a Heroic Life,* University of California Press, 1995

Tyler, P.: *Teresa of Avila, Doctor of the Soul,* Bloomsbury Press, 2013

Williams, R.: *Teresa of Avila,* Geoffrey Chapman, 1991